Guide to Becoming a Wall Street Programmer

How to become a Programmer on Wall Street. Make a ton of money by being close to the money. Minimize the stress and maximize the return.

By Alan White

Author Bio *5*

Why you should read this book *6*

Motivation *7*

Studying *9*

Getting the Interview *14*

Resume writing *17*

Passing the phone screen *19*

Passing the Interview *22*

Salary Negotiations *25*

Sample Interview, Responses, and Commentary *27*

FAQ *31*

Top Ten Tips and Takeaways *42*

Conclusion *43*

©Copyright 2016 Alan White - All rights reserved.

This document is geared towards providing exact and reliable information in regards to the topic and issue covered. The publication is sold on the idea that the publisher is not required to render an accounting, officially permitted, or otherwise, qualified services. If advice is necessary, legal or professional, a practiced individual in the profession should be ordered.

- From a Declaration of Principles which was accepted and approved equally by a Committee of the American Bar Association and a Committee of Publishers and Associations.

In no way is it legal to reproduce, duplicate, or transmit any part of this document by either electronic means or in printed format. Recording of this publication is strictly prohibited, and any storage of this document is not allowed unless with written permission from the publisher. All rights reserved.

The information provided herein is stated to be truthful and consistent, in that any liability, regarding inattention or otherwise, by any usage or abuse of any policies, processes, or directions contained within is the solitary and utter responsibility of the recipient reader. Under no circumstances will any legal responsibility or blame be held against the publisher for any reparation, damages, or monetary loss due to the information herein, either directly or indirectly.

Respective authors own all copyrights not held by the publisher.

The information herein is offered for informational purposes solely and is universal as so. The presentation of the information is without a contract or any guarantee assurance.

The trademarks that are used are without any consent, and the publication of the trademark is without permission or backing by the trademark owner. All trademarks and brands within this book are for clarifying purposes only and are the owned by the owners themselves, not affiliated with this document.

Author Bio

I choose to remain anonymous so that I can share what is really going on without impacting my career or my firm. Alan White is my pen name. I have been programming on Wall Street for over 15 years. I have a Graduate Degree from a prestigious US institution and have been working in some of the top investment banks and hedge funds. I have also passed the Chartered Financial Analyst (CFA) Level 1 exam to differentiate myself from other technologists.

I have interviewed over a hundred people during my career and have gone on many interviews often just for practice. I have read dozens of career coaching books and have seen a few career coaches. Many have sought me out for mentoring. They are fascinated by how my single mom raised me while living below the poverty line. They want to know how I worked smart and hard to get to where I am today. I will share with you what I learned the hard way. I wish I had this book many years ago as a college student.

I will share my tips on how to study, interview, get hired, and succeed as a Wall Street programmer.

The tricks that you will learn here will be applicable in any industry that you choose.

Why you should read this book

Hiring a career coach would easily cost $200 or much more an hour. I have summarized my hard-earned lessons here for you for a lot less. This book will give you a compounding return on investment. The earlier you put these lessons into play, the bigger your returns over your career.

Motivation

Why should you work on Wall Street?

By Wall Street, I am referring to the finance industry. We don't have to physically be in Wall Street or New York City. The answer is that the pay is one of the best. I currently work in a multi-billion dollar hedge fund and our top portfolio managers (PMs) make 7 figures ($1,000,000+). Those PMs need programmers to program all of their financial models, find Alpha (stocks and other financial instruments that will outperform the market), run their PnL (Profit and Loss), and a million other technical details. They can afford to pay top dollar for these results because they can't afford to worry about their systems making a mistake.

The money is great

As of 2018, as a fresh college graduate, you'll often start with $60K salary plus a $10-20K bonus with full benefits and two weeks of vacation. You can often make an extra $10-$15K per year as you gain more skills and experience. Senior programmers like myself are making a lot more without even being team leads. Senior programmers negotiate to get four weeks of paid vacation. We often get to WFH (Work From Home) for cable installations, emergency babysitting, doctors appointment, etc. The hours can be tough starting out but they can be much better as you can deliver high quality results in much less time.

As a junior developer, you're often stuck with a stressful job with an aggressive manager and you will often have to put in ten-twelve hour days. But, as you get more skilled, you can get a lot more done in a lot less time and have nine hour days and longer lunches. The best managers don't care so much about "face-time" (seeing your face in the office for long hours) to prove that you are getting things done. They care more about the results. As programmers, we hack our lives to get the most done in the least amount of time.

Studying

The easiest way to become a Wall Street programmer is get an Ivy League or other top school college degree in computer programming, mathematics, physics, engineering, or finance. If you don't have the fortune of coming from such a prestigious program, you can make up for it with other ways to show your skill such as the CFA (Chartered Financial Analyst) program, technical certifications, open-source projects, or other third-party verifications.

I recommend that you take the most challenging college major that you can. Wall Street respects the hard quantitative skills that you develop in the sciences like physics or chemistry. These translate very well into the mathematics, coding, and analysis skills that you will need. In any case, studying hard and having an excellent understanding of the lessons will help you go a long way.

Differentiating Yourself

To get to an elite level, you either have to be a rockstar programmer or a rockstar finance wizard. But, you can also get away with being an above average programmer AND have an average understanding of finance. There is such a huge demand for programmers who understand finance. It shows you plan to stay in this industry for a long time. You will save the company a lot of money because you won't need as many business analysts, senior programmers, or the business to explain the basics of finance to you.

College Graduates from Top Schools

If you are in a top school, leverage the alumni network, recruiting events, and college advisors to help you land your first job. These are invaluable. In the beginning of your career, focus on getting the experience and name-brand on your resume as opposed to the higher salary. You will make up more money over your total career.

College Graduates from Average Schools

You will have to work harder than graduates from top schools. Find out from your school if there are internship or volunteer opportunities in your field of study. Seek out mentorship programs or other alumni networking opportunities. Often from average schools, there won't be much of a network to help you. If you do have this network, take care of your network and treat them like gold. Make sure you send thank you notes and offer to help in any way you can. If you cannot land a job immediately, then work on some financial or technical certifications or study for the GMAT.

College Graduates from Below Average Schools

I have rarely seen a college graduate from a below average school. Unless you are the valedictorian or college president or have some other type of way to show your excellence, it will be very hard for you to begin a career on Wall Street. It's not impossible though but you will have to work harder to get to Wall Street. You have to want it badly. I recommend that you try to graduate well from a coding bootcamp. They will have networks to help you land a job if you work very hard.

College Graduates from Overseas

Banking runs 24/5 (24 hours a day, 5 days a week) and sometimes 24/7 (24 hours a day, 7 days a week). If you are overseas, you can get a great job doing support. Most banks keep software development in the US, and then the offshore team will support the systems overnight. You will learn a ton about the system and business. And during down times, have plenty of time to find other ways to add value. Those who work really hard and can deliver are often sponsored to relocate to the United States.

Choosing between a higher-ranked, expensive school and a lower-ranked less expensive school

One conundrum many students face is deciding whether a higher ranked school is worth the extra cost you might have to pay. My answer is definitely because:

1. Even though you will be paying more now, you will make up for that difference by a higher total income compounded over the years
2. The better school will have more opportunities for your first job and will get you an average of $5K -$10K more starting salary.
3. This then opens up to better jobs and opportunities over your career.
4. From a lower-ranked school, you might not even get to interview for the jobs that you want since those firms won't even recruit from there.
5. On average, even if you are an average student at the higher-ranked school, you will have more opportunities than being an above average student at the lower-ranked school. I found this out the hard way from going to a lower-ranked college but going to a higher-ranked graduate school. The recruiting events from the higher-ranked graduate school were amazing.

Getting the Interview

After you have your education, network all-the-time. Let everyone you know that you're looking for a job. I came from a mediocre college and an outstanding graduate school. The difference in getting a job is night and day.

Getting the Interview from a mediocre college

It was incredibly hard for me to get a job from a mediocre college. I emailed 100 job applications and I only got two responses. The first response was a scam and the second one was just a school trying to sell me something, It was incredibly disheartening. Finally, I emailed all of my friends and network my resume and asked for help. Fortunately, one in my network knew of an opening and I was able to get my first job. It was for a civil service job so was very far from Wall Street but it gave me a great foundation and first exposure.

Getting the Interview from an outstanding graduate school

Graduation from an outstanding graduate school was completely different. I even went to one job fair where all of the companies hiring managers were college alumni. They asked us to to rank the jobs that we liked the best. They said it was more of our choice as to where we wanted to work as opposed to whether they would hire us. This name brand school also helped me open quite a few doors on Wall Street.

Getting the Interview from LinkedIn

LinkedIn is an outstanding way to get your job. First you put in all of your info to make your online resume. You connect to as many people in your field that you can. This helps you gain social proof. Then you can start applying for jobs. Recruiters can often reach out to you.

Some LinkedIn Tips

1. Get a professional picture. You can pay about $50 for someone to take a professional headshot and they will get the lightning and occasional photoshop touch ups to make you look outstanding. I've seen some do miracles. This will help you get your foot in the door.
2. Customize your public profile URL
    a. You can easily create a name like www.linkedin.com/in/**yourname**
3. Ask for recommendations
    a. Social proof is huge. Recommendations could come from anyone and not just managers. Even professors who have complimented your work. Or customers from a freelance job.
    b. Fellow coworkers can recommend you as well. This shows you can get along well on a team.
4. Be professional on LinkedIn.
    a. Look at it like your official resume and corporate directory. Keep all of your politics and religion on other private and informal social networks.
5. Be very cautious about what you put on the internet and social networks. Many employers will Google and search your background extensively when making a hiring decision.

Resume writing

Resumes are absolutely critical to getting the interview. They should be 1-2 pages. You often don't need more than 2 pages because the interviewer doesn't need that much detail. The resume is to get into you into the interview. The interviewer can then ask you for more details. Minimize repeating yourself. Each job should show a growth progression.

Some resume writing tips

1. Include a professional email address.
    a. Something like yourname@foo.com It should be a professional name.
2. Don't include your full mailing address.
    a. Just your city and general location should be fine for extra security. People will contact you via email or phone.
3. You can include your linkedin custom public profile as mentioned in the linkedin section.
    a. This will separate you from most candidates since its rare that people do this. It also allows companies to see that you are thinking ahead.
4. If you have graduated in fewer than three years, then have your education at the top.
    a. If not, your education can be after your work experience; since your work experience will then be more relevant to your role.
5. Be confident almost to the point of bragging.

a. A resume is not the place to be humble. You want to look at yourself as a rockstar who can deliver the goods. Be confident about the value that you can bring. Sell yourself. Explain how you have helped each company.
   b. Ask someone else to write it for you. They should write your resume like they were marketing a car, investment, or other object that gives a great Return On Investment (ROI). Employers are looking at you as a ROI.
6. Be specific.
   a. Give actual numbers. I.e.
      i. Saved the company $10 million via project x,y, and z.
      ii. Generated $5 million in revenue via software x.
      iii. Cut critical query from one hour down to six minutes via query optimization.

Passing the phone screen

The phone screen is where you spend about half an hour to an hour getting to know the interviewer and the role. It's where you show why you are a good fit for the role.

Some tips for the phone screen
1. Get to a quiet place.
    a. If you are at home or have access to a quiet place, then this should be easy. But, if not, then you have to get creative. If you are already working or cannot get to a quiet place you can try:
        i. Booking a conference room at work during your lunch. You will have to avoid your team and manager like a ninja if you are at work.
        ii. Find a relatively quiet corner of a restaurant or café.
        iii. Find an indoor public area and walk around if necessary to find a quiet spot.
2. Research the company, the manager, and the role.
    a. The company could have a very bad reputation.
        i. Check out glassdoor.com and linked to see what others are saying.
    b. Research the manager.

        i. Is he - note I will also occasionally alternate with the female pronoun - a good person to work with? What is his reputation? Ask anyone you know.
  c. Research the role.
        i. Ask for a written job spec. Find out what metrics you will be measured on. What are the most important deliverables during the first six months. What are the ways to grow in the role?
  d. Write down any questions you may for the phone screen beforehand.

Starting the phone screen

  a. Always start with some small talk about the weather, how you are feeling, your commute into the office, etc. This helps relax the interviewer and see you as a human being with some personality.
  b. It's okay to ask for a salary range. A lot of jobs won't have a salary range so you could be wasting your time if they can't afford you. I recommend saying: "Just so that we're not wasting each others time, could you let me know the salary range".

During the phone screen
- a. Never interrupt. Always let her finish. Listen and reiterate your understanding.
- b. Do answer the question as quickly as possible. Interviewers have a day job and they want to know the answer quickly.

Ending the phone screen
- a. If you are interested, definitely let the interviewer know why. This will help you become memorable.
- b. Always have a few questions. If you don't you come across as uncaring about the job. Some good questions:
    - i. Can you tell me more about the
        1. Culture?
        2. Company Strategy?
        3. Technology Stack?

Passing the Interview

Preparing for the Interview

1. The best preparation is to ironically go on more interviews. When I am looking for a job, I apply to as many jobs as I can with the goal being to go on as many interviews as I can even if I don't intend to take the job. It in excellent and free practice.
2. Research the company and the role again. Find out its stock price, who the CEO and other leaders are.
3. Ask a friend to role play a tough interviewer with you. Record it via audio or ideally video and be very tough on yourself on how you could do better. Ask your friends for - honest and critical recommendations. Do not be defensive. Just understand and note what they are saying and improve yourself.
4. Bring a copy of your resume. The interviewer might have forgotten to print it out so this shows your consideration.
5. Find out what the dress code is. If in doubt, always wear business formal:
    a. For men: a suit and tie.
    b. For women: a suit, a jacket, and pants or a dress skirt.

Arriving at the Interview

1. Be in the area at least 15 minutes ahead of time. You can hang out at a nearby coffee shop or bookstore.
2. About 10 minutes before the interview, go through security. Make sure you have your photo ID. They often have to print out a security pass for you.
3. At the interview, feel free to ask for some warm water or to use the bathroom later. It's a great way to see what the kitchen and bathroom looks like. You will also get to see the office and other employees a bit more.

Starting the Interview

1. First impressions are critical. I often know within five minutes if a candidate is a great fit. So be on your best energy and behavior at the start. Stand up when offering a handshake. Lean forward slightly and smile as needed to show your interest in everything the interviewer has to say.
2. Take notes. This shows you are serious and interested.

During the Interview

1. You might have a technical test and a finance test. Relax and do your best. Do not argue if you feel the test is unfair.

2. Remember that the interviewer is often trying to figure out if:
   a. Can you do the job?
   b. Can you get along with the team?
3. So once you've proven that you can do the job, try to add some levity and humor to the interview. Remember that you are interviewing them as much as they are interviewing you. Ask a lot of questions to show that you want to make this a long term career with plenty of win-win growth opportunities.

Ending the Interview

1. Always ask questions even if they have answered all your questions. Interviewers are looking for this as an indicator of interest.
2. Reiterate your interest and ask the hiring manager when it's likely you will hear back from them. They could be interviewing a few other people or might have some Human Resources, budgeting, or other issues before making a decision.
3. If you are likely to receive or have received other offers, let the interviewer know. You can say this is my first choice, so I hope to hear from you soon. This is a great way to let the employer know you are valued and offers some social proof.

Salary Negotiations

Avoid giving away your salary history

1. A lot of companies and recruiters will ask for your salary history. It's an advanced move to not give this away. In New York City, it's actually illegal to ask for this because it has historically been a way to continually underpay historically underpaid minorities. I.e. once someone has been underpaid, and they continue to only make 10-20% more in their next job. This won't compound as well as someone who has been getting the same increases but has been paid fairly.
2. What if the employer requires this?
    a. There is no such requirement. They know how much value that you can bring. They will make an offer based on a salary range.

There are other things to negotiate besides salary

1. Along with the salary offer, you can also negotiate other aspects of the work. If they can't deliver on these as well, they might feel obliged to increase their offer further:
    a. Vacation Time
    b. Flex Working Hours
    c. Working From Home as necessary
    d. Continuing education and certifications

      e. Tuition Reimbursement

Sleep on it

1. Once you receive an offer, don't respond immediately. Say that you have to "sleep on it." It's a major decision that you would like to think about or discuss with your significant other.

Sample Interview, Responses, and Commentary

General Introduction

1. Tell me about yourself
   a. Tell us about coding, finance, and achievements
   b. I.e. I love programming and contribute to open source projects. I'm on Stack Overflow and have x,y,z certifications. I love the beauty of code. I also love finance and I invest in my portfolio on the side and buy and sell call options.
2. Why should we hire you:
   a. How do you differentiate yourself. Show some passion.
   b. I.e. I'm not only a technologist with an expertise in x,y, and z. I also understand the business and am took classes in finance, accounting, economics, etc. I work hard and stay late as necessary in emergencies. I have been on a 24/7 support rotation before. I have lead and managed these projects or teams.
3. What is your biggest strength
   a. Show passion in these answers so we know you're sincere, energetic, and confident.
   b. I.e. I like to understand the business and code thoroughly so that I solve a problem right the first time. This also

helps me build scalable code with little technical debt.
4. What is your biggest weakness
    a. What you describe here, you also want to describe how some can consider it a strength.
    b. You can describe past weaknesses and how you have overcome them and made them a strength.
    c. If they insist on a current weakness, you can describe it and your plans to make it a strength.
    d. Example 1: My last manager said my finance skills were weak so I purposely passed the CFA Level 1. I've read the Hull book on options.
    e. Example 2: My object-oriented programming skills used to be weak so I just passed the Java certification.
    f. Example 3: My Unix Scripting skills aren't as good as I like them to be so I have been studying up on it. Recently on my Ubuntu, I wrote a script that automated x,y, and z so that was a good exercise.

Technical

Practice for your specialty and according to the job description. Expect a written-test, whiteboarding, and oral explanations. There are hundreds of free websites on interview questions. Practice flashcards on Quizlet or Anki.

Finance

1. If you are a quant, then you will know these terms very well. If not, it's good to have a basic understanding of finance vocabulary. This shows your interest in finance and that you plan a long career in finance.
2. Some beginner terms; What's a:
    a. TVM
        i. Time Value of Money
    b. PV
        i. Present value - describes how much a future sum of money is worth today. It incorporates the TVM.
    c. NPV
        i. Net present value is the difference between the PV of cash inflows and the PV of cash outflows over a period of time. NPV analyzes the profitability of a projected investment.
3. Some advanced terms; What's a:
    a. CDS
        i. Credit Default Swap - A CDS is a credit derivative. It is similar to an insurance contract, providing

the buyer with protection against specific risks.
b. MBS
   i. Mortgage Backed Security - Asset-Backed Security (ABS) that is secured by a mortgage or collection of mortgages. The mortgages are sold to a SPV (Special Purpose Vehicle) that securitizes, or packages, the loans together into a security that investors can buy.
c. DV01
   i. Dollar Value 01 - A bond valuation calculation showing the dollar value of a one basis point decrease in interest rates. It shows the change in a bond's price compared to a decrease in the bond's yield.

FAQ

1. What's the difference between the Front Office (FO), Middle Office (MO), and Back Office (BO)?
    a. The Front Office is the money making and client facing portion of the business. You can make the most money here but be prepared to work long hours and have high stress.
    b. The Middle Office is direct support for the Front Office. MO handles Risk Management, Operations, compliance, project management and interfaces with the Back Office. There is decent salary and healthier work-life balance.
    c. The Back Office is everything else like Settlements, Infrastructure, and Human Resources.

2. If I have a choice, should I choose a technology role in the Front, Middle, or Back Office?
    a. If you're relatively young and can afford the stress and many hours to keep up with the Front Office, then definitely go for the Front Office. You can learn a lot and gain a great reputation. After two or

more years here, you can have many opportunities to go closer to the money (get into a trading or client-facing role) and make more money. Alternatively, if you want to take it easier, you can easily find an easier role in the Middle or Back Office without a significant loss in salary since your business experience and relationships will be very valuable. You will have proven yourself.

3. I have a choice of taking pretty much the same job at an Investment Bank and at a Hedge Fund. Which one would you recommend?
    a. I will generalize a bit here so that you get a basic understanding of my reasoning.
    b. Investment Bank
        i. Pros
            1. Generally, better name recognition to the public
            2. When you are settled in, you can generally relax more
        ii. Cons
            1. Can be very siloed. You might only need to know one limited set of technologies and business. You will get very deep into

one area to the detriment of others.
2. Lots of bureaucracy especially when it comes to change management and production releases.
3. Generally slower, new technology adoption

c. Hedge Fund
   i. Pros
      1. You are responsible for a lot more so you learn a lot more.
      2. You are not as siloed and can take on Business Analyst and other roles. This can be ideal if you want to go into management at a hedge fund or investment bank.
      3. Pay is generally better
   ii. Cons
      1. With the higher pay, comes higher expectations.
      2. Harder to just relax and collect a good paycheck.

d. Given the above, I would recommend a hedge fund. It's great exposure to a lot more technology and business so that you will learn more. There are many different types of hedge funds. Some smaller and newer funds take on a lot more leverage and risk so your job is at risk as well. Generally, this is okay, because you will have learned a lot and will have become more valuable as a result.

4. Can you tell me about some of the roles and in the order that you would recommend them?
    a. Software Engineer
        i. Making computers do amazing things means you will have an amazing career and salary. You can move onto other pure tech companies as well should you want to leave finance.
        ii. This can be very lucrative especially if you're in the hot technologies like artificial intelligence, business intelligence, big data, quantitative finance, and high frequency trading.
    b. Trade Support
        i. You would be interacting with the Front Office and have many opportunities to move into the Front Office or use technology to help them make more money and get a nice bonus as a result
    c. Project Manager
        i. If you can see big, complex, high NPV projects to completion; you will be very valuable. You can learn enough about the business and technology to move into upper management. You will

often have to become very strong in office politics.
   d. Business Analyst
      i. This is a very visible role and allows you to learn the business and write the requirements for the software engineers. Your hours are generally great with fewer deadlines and overnight support.
   e. Operations / Support
      i. These jobs are at risk of being offshored and automated. If you are a whiz at managing offshore teams or using code to automate these jobs, then this could be a great opportunity.

5. Should I take full stack dev role or be a specialist in a limited set of technologies?
   a. In the beginning of your career it's often best to get a full stack development role. You will become very valuable and you won't be bored because there's so much to do and learned. You will also learn more to be a manager where you have to be more of a generalist and understand every role on your team.

6. What is the lowest cost way to becoming a Wall St programmer?
    a. Generally, everyone has at least a college degree. So, if you were to go to a public school or a private school with a generous scholarship, then that would be very low cost. If you studied a ton on your own and mastered your skill set, that would be significantly more valuable than the name-brand of your college.

7. What technologies should I study?
    a. Generally the hottest technologies now and in the foreseeable future would be:
        i. Artificial Intelligence
        ii. Data Science
        iii. Big Data
        iv. High Frequency / Low Latency Trading
        v. Business Intelligence
    b. For less cutting edge but pretty much universally valuable
        i. Object Oriented / high-level language Programming (Java, C#, Python, etc)
        ii. Scripting languages (Perl, Powershell, Unix Shell Scripts, etc)
        iii. SQL (Structured Query Language)
        iv. Excel VBA - an amazing amount of business is done in high finance via Excel

8. What should I look for in a manager?
   a. Remember, when you are interviewing that you are also interviewing them. If you've build enough rapport, ask if your manager would like to share some of her background. How long she has been running a team? (A less experienced manager might not be as emotionally intelligent). How many people are on her team? What's her management style? What will she expect from you in the first and second year?
   b. You will want to be sure that you get along well since you will be spending a lot of time together.
   c. If your manager isn't willing to share that info with you, study her body language. Does she look you in the eye and treat you with respect?
   d. I had a hiring manager make me wait one hour before an interview. That was incredibly disrespectful and also a sign of how disorganized he was. He knew I was there but never came into apologize or explain why he was late. In hindsight, I'm glad he didn't make an offer because I likely would have hated working with him.
   e. I had another hiring manager not look me in the eye during the interview. There were red flags on his body

language but I wanted the job badly because it was a role that give me an opportunity to learn a really hot technology. Foolish me. I was absolutely miserable there. I didn't really learn that much because I was so stressed out, and I left that company very quickly.

9. What should I look for in a team?
   a. You will want to see if it's a good team atmosphere. Are the teammates pleasant. Will they help bring you up to speed and be cool to hang out with?

10. How can I increase my confidence during the interview?
    a. You can "fake it until you make it"
    b. Know that you can figure out any task that they give you even if you have to spend 10+ hours a day working on it.
    c. Know that you are willing to work hard until you become an expert in your field.

11. What free resources would you recommend?
    a. https://www.wallstreetoasis.com is a great free site to get a feel for the high finance culture and vocabulary
    b. https://www.tutorialspoint.com/index.htm has some amazingly great technology tutorials free of charge.

Top Ten Tips and Takeaways

1. Being a Wall Street Programmer is the best of high finance and programming.
2. You can go into any other industry after being at this elite level
3. Differentiate yourself by being adept at both programming and finance. Or majoring in one and minoring in the other.
4. Add measures and brag truthfully in your resume.
5. Always ask questions during the phone screen and interview.
6. Go to as many interviews and interview role-plays as you can.
7. Record yourself with audio and ideally video during your practice interviews.
8. Never give away your salary history. You will often undervalue yourself.
9. Negotiate vacation time and other assets besides salary.
10. Relax: You are interviewing them as much as they are interviewing you.

Conclusion

It has been a pleasure writing this book for you. Many of these lessons I have learned the hard way. I hope this has been a great investment of your time and energy.

If you have found this book helpful, please recommend it to a friend and leave a review.

Best wishes with your career whether it is on Wall Street as a programmer or wherever it may be.

www.ingramcontent.com/pod-product-compliance
Lightning Source LLC
Chambersburg PA
CBHW031504210526
45463CB00003B/1074